Poems
for the
LONESOME

Poems
for the
LONESOME

Warren Miles

Sarah Erlund

ShortStack Publishing, LLC
ShortStackPublishing.com

2 3 4 5 6 7 8 9 10 IS 26 25 24 23

ISBN: 978-1-0881-8334-2

Library of Congress Control Number: 2023937936

This book is for everybody sometimes,
Somebody every time,
and any other time anybody
feels a little lonesome

Table of Contents

When in there

You're underneath your skullcap
and your scalp under your hair

and you simply must be careful
what you let in
when in there

We us all
the source of heaven
headed into atmosphere

Have a hell of an attachment
to the terrible
we fear

Some can call it meditation
Some introspection
Others prayer

We are built to work and look in
to the feelings that we feel

There are rods and cones inside there
where you're seated in your head

They act like a projector
for the light that you let in

Or the dark and cold and hardness
or the warmth and joy and cheer

We then paint with that our memories
which we remember, unaware

of the changes that we implement
each time we run the tape

of the time we had a better time
or plan or an escape

We are so complex perplexing and
we complicate that all

With our lexicon of feelings
that we express or often swallow

Shallow we are water
if spread thin
we can't break fall

and if found in
over our depth too long
we often drown with sorrow

Because we're all under a skullcap
and a scalp under some hair

and while plotting escape
we have to watch

All that's let in
when in there

props

The reasons I feel like giving up
is there's a lot that I can't stop
I wish that things were different
other things I wish were not
Every wave will crash
and it's a choppy sea we're caught in
Maybe I speak too much
but there's a lot that I've forgotten
or don't mention
We've been clenching hands up
Stomachs balled in knots
Giving up on caring more
This carousel we all need off
It's a charade and it's a shell
and it's a snare in which we're caught
and it's apparent we aren't well
We play for real but feel like props

Chase the dopamine

Too much woe in me
where the warmth is supposed to be
Sometimes feel like loneliness has chosen me
Spirit so broken
Once it's exposed they'll see
I've been told that all scars heal
but these ones won't for me
Trying to start each day I'm facing
more hopefully
Get closer to those that hold
and keep the cold from me
and draw distance from those who soak up
what I own from me
or break me up inside
and take the soul from me
Some creatures survive by living socially
but I've been lone wolf living
so I know the scene
When your only human interaction's
getting groceries
You can't find any traction
There's no openings
to join up with a faction
without code-switching
to pretend you're after more
than just a social scene
and then depending on the factors
like the quotes you read
and your clothing and your background
Chase the dopamine

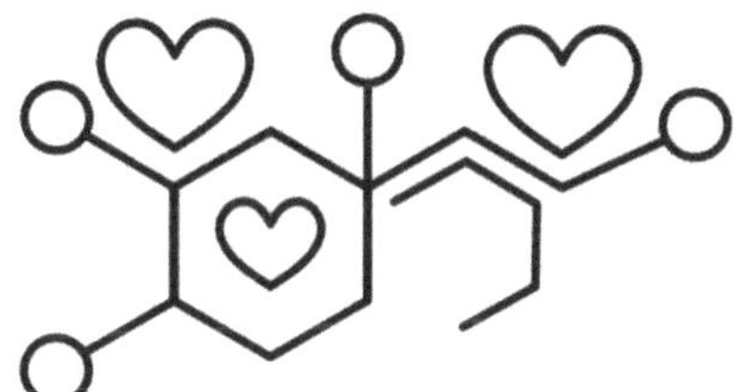

heroes

Never meet your heroes
cuz you'll never really know them
Heroism isn't men and women
it's a moment
of inspiration from beyond
An instrument is chosen
and given chance to act designed
before it's bent or broken

a message from a distant future

I breathe man-made oxygen
photosynthesized by man-made plants
synthesized on a man-made station made
from a madman's man-made plans
Men and Women on a maiden voyage
Nano Machines in them so advanced
Through some simple bio symbiosis
alchemically they all dance
So far from home and comfort
Out for what could come at last
As they float toward oasis
in deep spaces endless sands
Trigger finger species
Hunger never-ending
Always for the taking
Broken now depending
upon the lonesome vessel-
garden at the threshold
Of the reach of understanding
cuz we think we're special
Living for survival
Broken tip of pencil
We can never ride or write back home
Wish it was that simple

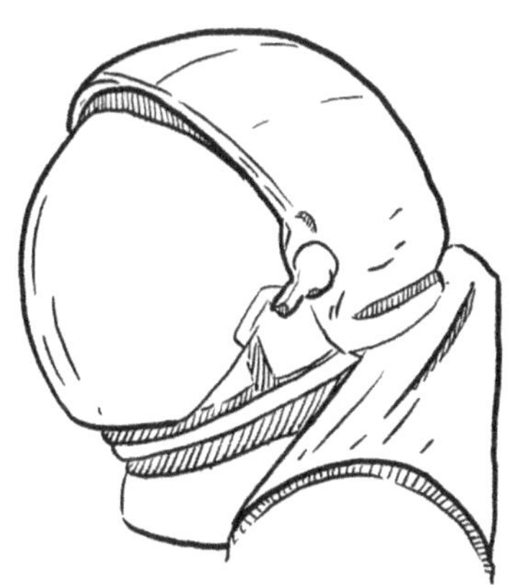

The want back

I want back every moment
that was taken once you made me hurt
I yearn to know who and what that boy
you changed could have loved or would
have preferred
Wish that I could escape the haze
that lays over my eyes
and this crazy world
But once you laid your hand on me hard
My light died while my body burned
You picked me up and choked me
and you beat me with closed fists
You told me to tell no one
or they'd take away us kids
and due to life's past drama
foster care and evictions
I became a coward with my voice
while you swung and landed hits

No chance at consistency
other than changing scenery
I escaped you at least physically
But can tell this is not the real me
Wish I could work back through the scars
and misplaced thoughts and broken heart
and ask that kid what he would want
When he becomes a man

Because now I sit here at a loss
An echo of the hurt you caused
I can't imagine being a father
because mine left me mishandled

Now I wander lonely roads
and shrug off rain and biting cold
Was once a part of something holy

Now just alone
and missing home

I hope to one day fill the cracks
you left in me and take it back;
the life I lost the way the path
That first time that you hit me, Dad

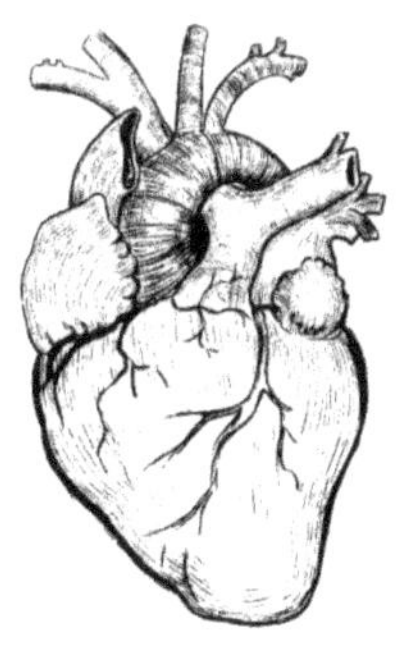

Puzzle

I feel necessities jumbled
as I run through the jungle
With all our love for the struggle
We have forgotten the subtle
All this complexity's muzzled
internal structures we all build
We either mute or expose ourselves;
missing piece of the puzzle
Criticism a toll booth
You try to do what you're told to
by those that don't really know you
or who respect what you go through
Intentionally they misquote you
Contextually crucify you
and then admit after some time
that they never did like you
Other option's find likeness
in those that share your excitements
and amplify all of your efforts
at real peace and alignment
to yourself as a spirit
back to your inner child
A wonderment not quite yet of this world
We protect till we die old
It's not a thing worth denying
this ain't about your religion
or how you lack it

It's about the way
you make your decisions
Do you wake in the morning
with a strong sense of wonder?
Or do you take and take
no matter what's destroyed
while you plunder?
Do you have sense of justice?
Do you crave love and affection?
Or are you out for your bottom line
Snorting lines for sensation?
I'm not here to give guidance
I'm merely asking some questions
for where I come from
it's gravity and time
that teach us our lessons
You simply must be receptive
to what's meant by temptations
as we navigate the Aether-sphere
and wane to a crescent

Warren

Fingers gloveless
so she can feel me when I touch her
Streets I'm in love with
vest decked in buckles
Burning rubber
Less hype and humdrum
More cut and dry and clever
Had a lot of cold nights
but unaffected by the weather
They can't breathe my atmosphere
so I don't let them near me
From out of this stratosphere
but here for you presently
Even rigid trigger fingers
can fall, fail, or hesitate
Lot of us living life
in the past tense
in the present state
Lot of us living off of the last mans
last dinner plate
Halls of the fallen calls
demanding
We remember inner hate
I'm just a man and his hands
not here to overcompensate
for what came before
and pretend I have the recipe

Warren the streets
Warren in jungles
Warren us all
When we're in the hustle
Wearing us out
Working out our muscles
Warping our words
When we need a rescue
what can we do?
I'm trying to ask you
There's Warren in the valleys
Warren the mountains too
Mom called me Warren
but I'm tired of fighting through
all of this war
Unwarranted
All we do

Mascara and secrets

You can see her sad eyes
glisten in the sequins
Sings her little heart out
Drinking every weekend
Sure has had a hard life
Look at her you see it
Cover up the bad lines
Mascara and secrets

Smokes another cigarette
Says she thought of quitting
So hard to remember when
there's so much worth forgetting
As she downs another shot
backlit by a city
Silly little broken heart
Will she wilt
or get free?

Holding on for someone else
that just may never show up
Golden strings on her guitar
She struggles just to hold up
As all her emotions swell
to musical crescendo
Cast a siren sonnet spell
that nobody will notice

Hard pill

From the voting booth to the body bag
The whole country's screwed
and we're all attached
to the downward spiral that's come to pass:
They don't care for us and they never have
On quarantine we can see it clear
Their mask is off as we breathe the air
that we all pollute as they loot and clear;
No warranty just horrid fear
Don't see a doc
you'll face a bill
You aren't sick at all
if you say you're well
Just fake the smile to save the face
of the land you love as we grab and take
Fuck gravity if you're to fall
it's all your fault
So don't dare to call
on us;
Because
We're just you after all
and you're all US
Hard pill to swallow

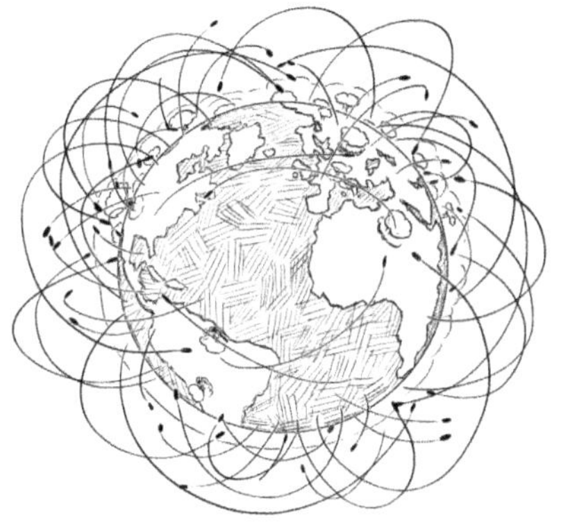

wisp of a ghost

Days gone by flicker in the fireplace
Now it hurts to try; you just fly in place
Miss the time when you could fry in peace
On a seaside night or quietest days
You look to them and admire the pace
but look down hard
when you eyed how it's made
We get pulled apart
all we write all we say
Its a wisp of a ghost
that's been tired of today
All the calm in the pain
as we call and exclaim
from the bowels of our breaks
that no coward could claim
We hold power we wield
and we watch and we wait
for occasion for words
like a cowl or a cape
We can heal we can break
weaken locks on the chains
of the hearts of the hardest
who are parting with ways
with the toxins inside them
The thoughts so they say
are the wolves that we feed
if we want all our pain
to be put into those all around us who can't
keeping on grasping at straws just to not
understand

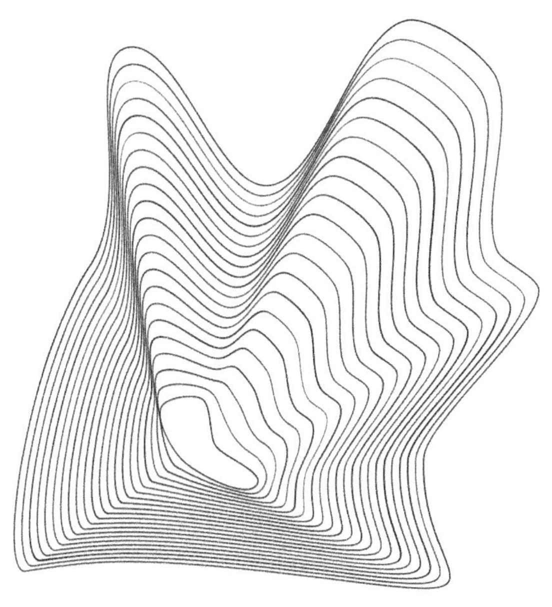

Talk

Step away from your pain
Leave it next to the door
Let's head outside again
It's time to explore
There's a whole world out there
Every wave and contour
is waiting for you
What are you waiting for?
See the nature in things
Really all that there is
is a whole lot of love
and a whole lot to miss
but we gotta choose wise
because time will catch up
and so will our lies
and our cover-ups
So put down your pain
Come with me let's explore
I know that it is hard
but it's hard to ignore
the ticking inside us all
that one day will stop
I know that you're broken
So am I
so let's talk

dispel

I hope if you're casting magic
that you cast it in my favor
Though it's something you may not see;
it is something I will say here
I have been through endless turmoil
have too much on my plate here
to make my way through hexes, spells, and
incantations that you make here

Visiting

Feel I'm not from this dimension;
that I'm just here for a visit
but I feel I brought a message
This my chance I'm gonna seize it
May I please have your attention
as we sing along to treason
There's a lot they wanna take from us
for some damn made-up reason
I refuse apologies
let's move the cogs
go on and grease them
Time has passed
and all this rust is thoughts
we often keep on thinking
over worth we're meant to offer
or the purpose in all meetings
how we each of us are chords
in one harmonious receiving
how we gather scars and wrinkles
and some have hairlines receding
and then try to hide all those awards
and miss out on their meaning
I would give to you some peace and joy
and a hopeful hug upon our meeting
because nobody is from this world
just visiting, then leaving

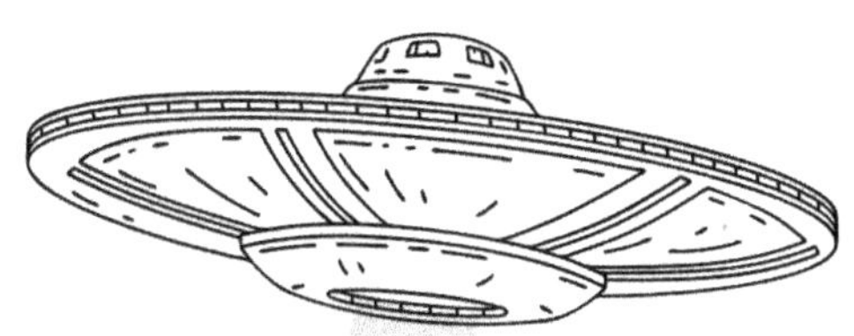

Möbius strips

Some think like Möbius strips
and wear infinity scarves
Worry on suffering cows
while the community starves
I think like Robin Hood did
I'll take from rich for the poor
and Nottingham won't touch me
cuz I'll never pull over
I think they've woven a yarn
that they've pulled over our eyes
using our tendency to care
for show and tell
and the size
of the homes of our neighbor
or luxury they afforded
Now with magic mirror in your palm
they watch and record it
It's a place you'd rather be
if you just had the time or funds
or could drop all obligations
Hobble off into the sunset
It's the fear you have to swallow in the
aftermath of all this
Living hard and loving fast
and trying not to lose your polish
It's epiphany in loss of friends
Its pitfalls in your progress
Quite impossible to pocket
all the ways the teaching tosses

all the mistakes and the makeups
It's those things that never were
It's the giving out of healing
as you're looking for your cure

It's the all of us just out here trying not to
feel defeated
as we trample each other in traffic
flying down the freeway
It's that second inside all that
when you hear your favorite song
and you take a breath and let it go
then tune out and move on
It's a lot it's next to nothing
it's all pay per view per visit
It's a moment and it's gone
and now it's memory

Or is it?

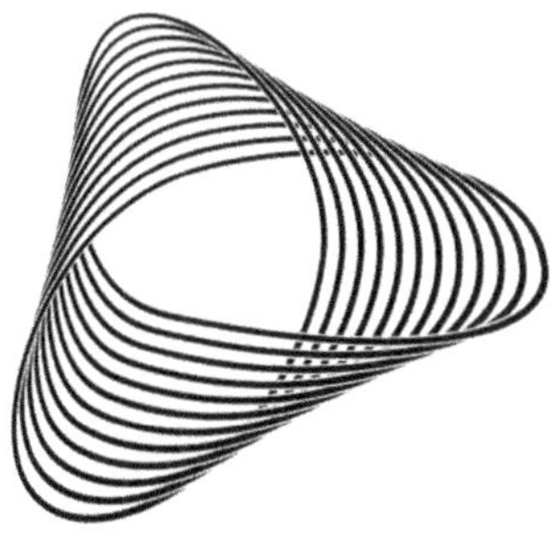

unconditional love

The planets overpopulated
I'm over being popular I hate it
for she so loved her own creation
that she allowed them to
enforce enslavement
She allowed to them too;
their torture and hatred
She spared no expense
on their threshold for pain
and
when they were weak and wrong
and all broken and lame
She loved them so deeply that
she left them that way

Virtually there

So close I could touch you
I don't want to or care
Living in the future like I'm virtually there
Soft skin of my fingertips your curves are so fair
Loving you through internet I'm virtually there
Pills they put up in me
left me underprepared
Fuck it pop another and I'm virtually there
Link me up with doctors
with heads filled up with air
and get me to my cloud 9
Now I'm virtually there

Monsters we've been making
barbed and horned and horny
Swallow all the smut and filth engross us all in
porno
Act as though resolve comes when we look away
ignoring
All the issues that we let out when at home and
all alone
Holy Moses jumping jacks
its a flesh-fest hocus pocus
The way the wave gets let in
is akin to plague's of locusts

Making out like bandits
as we climax to a close
They just want a dime for every time we try and
blow our loads
Bogus global holdout
as some try to hold it in
Others acting hard up
better smart up to their scent
its the oldest form of art
but now it's how attention's spent
whether trying to ignore it
or just letting it all in

So close I could touch you
I don't want to or care
Living in the future like I'm virtually there
Soft skin of my fingertips
your curves are so fair
Loving you through internet I'm virtually there
Pills they put up in me
left me underprepared
Fuck it pop another and I'm virtually there
Link me up with doctors
with heads filled up with air
and get me to my cloud 9
Now I'm virtually there

Zombies we are breeding
they are cold and so unfeeling
Medicate away our worries
We're ignoring what we're fearing
Coming true its all around us
it's a plague but its been scripted
by the doctors who don't do their jobs
just act so damned indifferent
whole world; no libido
but we got antidepressants
and we also have no regard
for its affect on our presence
You get nervous for the future
so they prescribe you a xanax
There's a pill these days for any way
that life can create panics
And we zone out on the tv
in our cognitive dissonance
As we're eaten alive by systems
that only need our components

So close I could touch you
I don't want to or care
Living in the future like I'm virtually there
Soft skin of my fingertips your curves are so fair
Loving you through internet I'm virtually there
Pills they put up in me
left me underprepared
Fuck it pop another and I'm virtually there
Link me up with doctors
with heads filled up with air
and get me to my cloud 9
now I'm virtually there

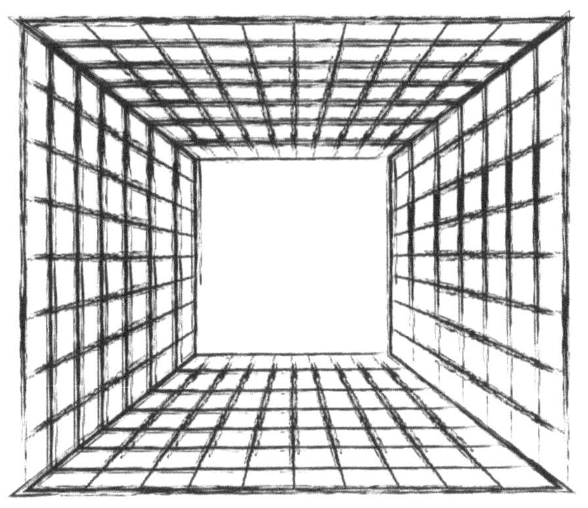

Skeletons 4 sale

Skeletons tread in the closet of the pompous
It's been a hell of a ride and we aren't even on yet
Riveting pivots, to critique and tease for profit
Digital prints to film disease
and to fill pockets
The bliss is abysmal;
Demi-gods of the hustle
we piss in the wind
as they whistle on and shuffle
and cut swift with the quickness
that slices down to the muscle
and then eat it all up
and enjoy every morsel
Each moment the first
even if its rehearsal
We get what we give
if we think from the torso
If we leave what we take
We will get even more so
You can hide who you are
but can't hide from the hearse, though

Curious fury

Itch I've gotta scratch
I've got a curious fury
I wonder why sometimes it is
I clench these fists that I carry
They said to me it's cuz I'm holding
so much unresolved hurt in
but every time I try to sort it out
Here comes a new whirlwind
I been growing in and out
Have been from hither to thither
and everywhere I go
Seems they simply cannot handle the ether
Isopropyl alcohol
here comes the cleanest of stingers;
this next line:
We all some day become
whichever demon we feed first

Love made

Hope you know that you are made of love
and you are loved
Everything's a pretty circle stacked together
all at once
We just experience it in moving moments,
Interruptions, and eruptions
While out here trying hard to learn
the way the aether functions
I'm so happy for your presence
and our pleasant intersections
I couldn't be more happy
with our interactions and their lessons
That anyone could turn from light you bring
to me is like a stabbing
Any shadows should stop a haunting and
get their bags and get to packing
Because I now have your back
so over you they have no power
and you're worth the effort
Flesh to vapor rain
to daily shower
So, if you have to cry, darling
you can lean right against my shoulder
Nobody is going to harm you long
now that we have each other

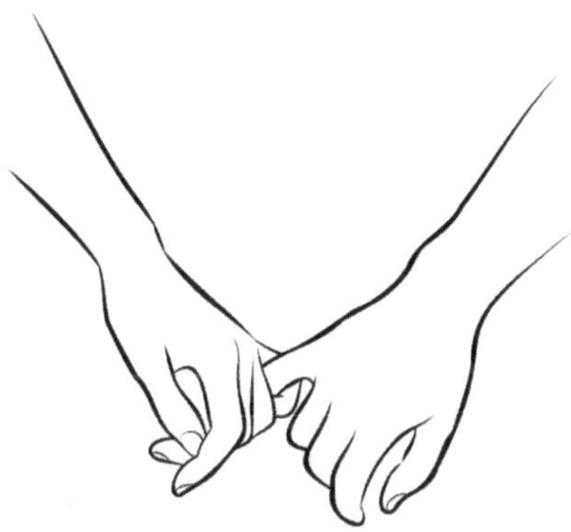

A prayer to the sea

As I stand on top of sands
that understand not what I've done
I'm reminded of who I am as I watch the
setting sun
I may not be from this land but it's about
how it's run
Itself into the ground
The beat down become numb
I beckon to the beaches
to now see us as we are
Seasons change and reasons too
release us from your guard
Let your healing waters flood us
over each and every pore
Pour your welcome cold into vessels
only lesser men explore
Please just flood us all soon
in forgiveness from a god
One that cares an awful lot
but just cannot bear to watch
As we fornicate and laugh with glee
A changing of our costume
doesn't hide the pleasure that we feel
in suffering and exhaustion
of the lesser than us that we feed off
please just free us all
We need your frigid feeling energy
to be cool with this all

Superbabe

Somewhere deep in an artic cave
is a super girl
I wish would save me
Out of this world
with laser rays
that shoot out her eyes for days and days
Like kryptonite she makes me weak
I dream about her when I sleep
From somewhere way past mercury
Mercurial and it's hurting me
Defender of the Milky Way
The way she moves her super legs
Out of my league
and in the scene
to smash the villains face and spleens
Wish I knew her secret identity
I'm no Lois Lane though,
so woe is me
She's my sultry super soldier queen
but I know she'll never notice me

Pickets and Sigils

Either live your life
or try to sell it
Whole ride we're on
so psychedelic
We just slide along
it's kinda silly
Companionship sails
in the silent distance
and the load it bears
are the timely lessons
That one may receive
if accepting blessings
but you could pass by
if you're insides twist in
At their very sight or
At sigh in breathes wind
We can watch the sky
as the stars that glisten
act as a guide to our wiles
and wishes
As the moon in the night dances
wax to a crescent
We get wrecked on the inside
then act as though less than
We wrap ourselves up
like presents for Christmas
and hope that burned bridges
smoke signals forgive us

then settle on down to irregular livings
outside of the boundaries
of pickets and sigils
Inside cries they let out
at our funerals and vigils

its the unobvious
but then often apparent
As we search for ourselves
in the eyes of our parents
So either live your life
or try hard to sell it
Whole ride we're on so psychedelic

plastick

There's plastic inside everything
There's plastic in the sea
Now there's plastic inside every being
There's plastic inside me
We made it all from plastic
in some egoistic plea
Now ulcerative cancer's
been a reoccurring theme
It can hold your cans together
but it can't do everything
See it takes ten lives to break down
and there's microscopic beads
of it floating in the ocean;
which the fish begin to eat
and then guess what
we're chomping on
when we go eat sushi
Circumstance has gotten worse somehow
they've found it in the beef
at the same time climate breakdown
has us worried for the bees
Don't know how we're supposed to turn back
It's in everything we see
In a fake world full of plastic
with no cure or way to leave

Elaborate Decorating

I see past the complications
to transpose my compositions
Don't care about condemnation
I'm the coldest on the playground
On a mission they should stay down
once I knock them on their asses
This is not a poem or rap song
This is scripture; here's a passage:
While you fools massage your egos
I get better in the darkness
I will never fear my shadow
and you're running from the carnage
that you've wrought with past mistaking's
so it's happiness you're faking
Watching as the walls now crumble
Such elaborate decorating
Decadent the delay
you deluge on the decaying
Taking by default
and plain old overcompensating
While you undercompensate those
in your employ that you're paying
You're terrible
This ain't a game, and I was never playing
Prayerful thoughts that coexist with hateful rhetoric
Misread messages from God
now all are Heretic
Terraform your territory
so nothing can live
upon its surface
without permission:

Hostile narrative
Architecture made to dissuade
the beat down or homeless

We've become the monsters
that we used to fear
When we were kids
Even the best among us have
cognitive dissonance
emptiness that's in your hearts:
commerce and businesses

this doesn't rhyme but it remembers

The idea is that we are all at this edge between
infinite space and distance
and also are sucked against
absolute crushing weight and closeness
The magic of this dimension
is everything happening between

Movement in chaos
is a grand illusionary pattern
that is disrupted
once any of the chords of harmony
are struck or resonated
at any of the perceptively infinite irradiating
nodes that this unending struggle has
through its supreme design itself generated
to nod back in agreement at its own presence
We are nothing but clusters of this agreement
between the absolute and the obsolete
We are the hope of another breath not afforded to
that which would invent breath to lose it
As much is shown to us through music and dance
and art and expression; like a prism to light
but then focused back in:
Let each hue reflect a lesson

a nice greeting

Remind me if we've met before?
You're beyond my favorite metaphor
May be impolite but I know for sure
I have seen your eyes in another world
Can only stand for myself and word
but could swear I've met your face before
As we face this metamorphosis
Yours is fierce and peerless and gorgeous
Could have thought I swore some oath
somewhere before
when mean meant most
But, if I didn't
forgive my showing
that I like your look
and where this is all going

Sea of lonely

Math is bad
trying to make a difference out here
and some they get subtracted
Ignore it
add in the distractions
on the screens we glance at
pretty up the tragic
Pandemonium Metropolis
Neo-gothic
loathsome manic
I'm in love with the geometry
but the formula brings madness
Feel a lump in my esophagus
I reach down to deliver
divine message from a better me
before I was a sinner
Sit atop the roofs
I watch over
a seascape full of lonely
If I left or died tomorrow
most would pretend they didn't know me
No apologies no worries
feel the soreness in the joints now
Though we used to pass around a joint
that fun isn't a choice now
If we dared to cross the barriers
that life has put between us
would we all be too obscene
or be glad someone else could see us?
Is the honest what we ask for
or do we prefer the sweetness?

Is there too much tart
in the very hard
to let guard down and
be seen as we are?
Or is this a game where someone will keep score?

Guess we'll know, or not
just like we never were;
when we return to whatever
it was we were before

Skinny depth

Your eyes remind me of ponds
I once swam in as a child
So crystal clear, pretty, ponderous,
wonderful, and wild
I'd love to get to know you
and maybe spend a while
learning about your nature
What kind of creature lives inside you?
Any mind an ecosystem
and yours has my fascination;
If I cast a line to catch a wish,
will I catch it?
Or be left waiting?
Either way that blissful wait
and view of scenery I take in
is the perfect get away
from any turmoil I'm facing

Monster, becoming

Love the world I'm living in
sometimes I can't believe it
The planet's boiling over
and there's people thanking Jesus
The homelessness, and turmoil
is SO ever persistent
that the wealthiest among us
head to space for risk assessment
I love every tree, and flower,
bird, and bee, and all are dying
We can purchase clothes
from mobile phones
while starving kids are crying
What I love the most of all though,
is we are all no longer hiding
that we only care about ourselves
and don't care for the climate
Now, we still sure will tweet about
how temperatures are climbing
but only from the angle
of its effect on the timing
with alignment to vacation plans
While ocean level's rising
eats away slowly at every coast:
the cost of all our flying

Cowabunga buddy!
I just love all our consumption!
How lush jungles are now barley fields,
because that's what cows are munching
Rad how oceans floor is barren,
fish are stupid!
let's make fun of them!
sushi's too delicious
and it's just ourselves we're running from
Every beast leaves waste for sure
and humans, we're a cunning one
We forget: We are the place
that all the pain is coming from
and we cannot change our habits
and we will not give up one of them
We're the demons in the hell we made
If you can't beat them
try becoming them

Circus

Has surviving been worth it?
I've been told that no one's perfect
All your pain you don't deserve it
Still they dish it out and serve it
So many forces here on earth that
affect our focus and our service
to ourselves and to our purpose
I propose it's all a circus

Baby bird

I found a little baby bird
that had a broken wing
The little baby bird was scared
she'd never fly or sing
So I held the little baby bird
to help to ease the sting
Told my baby bird
that every fall
leads to a better spring
Accidents happen in life
to most all little birds
Sometimes we are left with scars
to show what we have learned
and the process of our healing
brings a certain introspection
and the more that we ignore that fact
the less the lessons lessen
I know that for myself
and so I'll always guard your heart
even once you fly above the clouds
and sing to moon and stars
Then we both can laugh about
these frustrating painful parts
I love you so much little baby bird
Your healing growth is art

perpetuation

We are the planet's skin
Gotta exfoliate
All of us are kin
It's not up for debate
Even the forsaken
have a time and a place
in the tapestry we live in:
Three-dimensional space
All can learn from observation
whether psycho or empath
It's an open conversation
You too can have an impact
See, the plane we're on is designed
with the pitfalls and setbacks
to perpetuate our energy:
You get what you give back
and you'll lose what you take here
All the fools and the fake here
attach to any shiny thing these days
that calls itself "savior"
It's a ruse it's a shame we're
being held back to wait here
by the most ignorant among us
Devils do advocate here
It's a mess so we're sinning
while the worst of us, winning
pretend the whole thing isn't going down
then drown in indifference

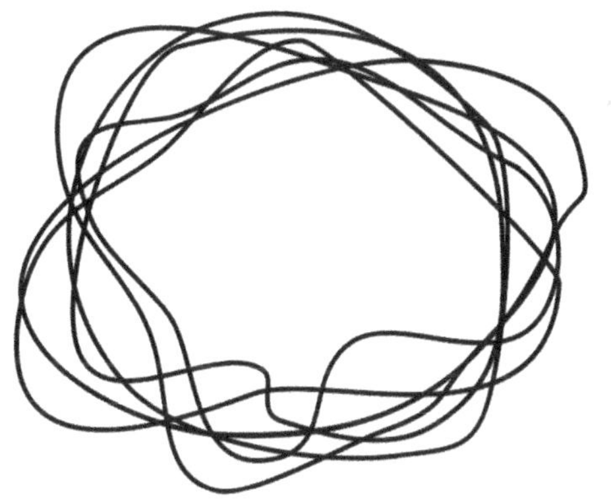

Time

We should be meditating
instead of mating
All wet and waiting
for medication
Our destination
is predicating
so we penetrate
in fluctuations
Capacity
at max or vacant
Luck that's run-up
Dusty basements
We act as though we're not adjacent
to door of death
who is lacking patience
but we just laugh
and fan the flames that
burn the homes of souls so ancient
For they say time is cold; complacent
but I feel calmed by all the ways it
shows the truth to eyes that face it
and melts away the lies and fake shit
So do take some; if you can take it
fore it takes us; all as we watch and waste it

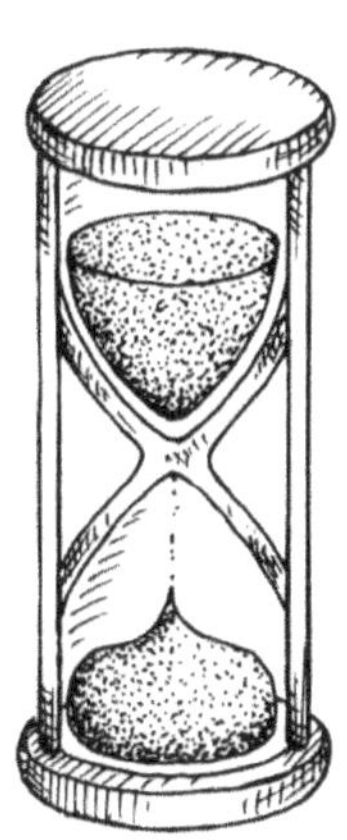

dirty filthy

Nasty dirty filthy crazy
that's what they been calling me
but I just need them off my case
while I fulfill this prophecy
The arguments ad hominem
It's herbivorous pondering
I'm saying that it has no teeth
to say the time you're squandering
in our ever changing moving world
upon which most are wandering
would be better spent if you just focus
on what to buy
and not your dreams

The Infection

It's a drought in Colorado
and there's flooding in Vegas
We won't change our direction
until the path is too dangerous
It's already too late
and now look at your faces
Focused on your smart phones
Stuck in virtual spaces
Whole worlds gone to feces
as the infection sets in
Investment in crypto
like the bro-est of brethren
While the west coast burns in front of us
You'll have no protection
but I guess if you just pray enough
you'll get into heaven

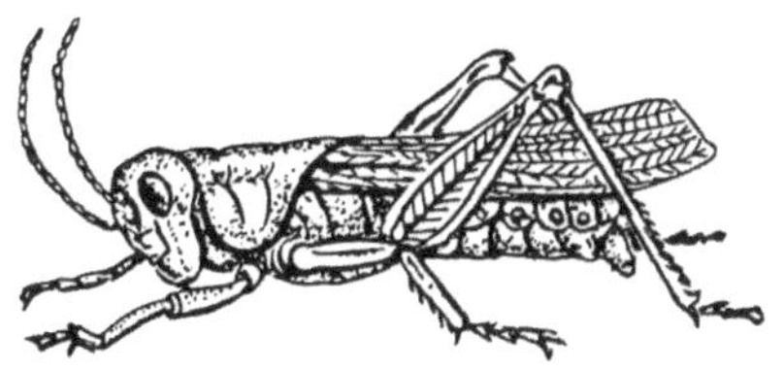

Conduit

The body is a conduit
through which a soul lives 3D
on the mortal plane
I'm sort of saying
we're broadcasts on a tv
that we tend to call a planet
because looks can be deceiving
and perceptions can be bent like light
when you're the one whose beaming
And we're beamed in like a signal
from a nice computer tower
using the latest 8k UHD reception viewing power
Made to give us pristine picture
of our open-world adventure
With the graphics turned to ultra
and a story at its center
One of helpful friends and NPCs
to lead you through the lonely
or the empty or the unfriendly
or heavily foreboding
It's where most are born to family
with only some worth knowing
We don't get to pick a class or even
choose perks while we're growing

Some are pricks and bullies though
so we all get pricked and bullied
because resolution isn't
given to every player fully
and you play your best to love and learn
and navigate the coding
and you get so damn immersed
that you forget that you've been pulled in
from a place that is beyond the worst
inside a massive hard drive
that we call our multiverse
it's our reception to the swan dive
that is then inverted
Not perverted; it's a combo gift and curse
The question is though:
When it's over,
will you be who you were at first?

daffodil

I love you little daffodil
Adore your look
and way you feel
I'm just a dork and no big deal
but a whiff of you
and I am well
When season's hard
your petals heal
you move with winds
and bring good will
could pick you, sure,
but I'll just sit still
I love you little daffodil

The tree

I'm just a tree that never fruits
always so misunderstood
Read the papers and the notes
always try to do what's good
History will read my quotes
and will see under the hood
all the shadows that I form
Must be me and not my movement
I'm just a tree that never fruits
How could I be a bad or good one?
I'm still made of wood and roots
Were my actions not the true ones?
I grew leaves that took in sun
Doesn't that amount to something?
I took in nourishment and loving
Does it now amount to nothing?
Why must I be uprooted?
I'm a tree that never fruits
I'm reliable as ever; I have every other use
I present myself to hold, and to protect you
from abuse
from the elements you face
and face it: weather is obtuse
It will disregard your favors
Me? I take them in and use
every itty bitty gesture
Dry your hair and let it loose
while you're underneath my branches
I'm the tree that never fruits

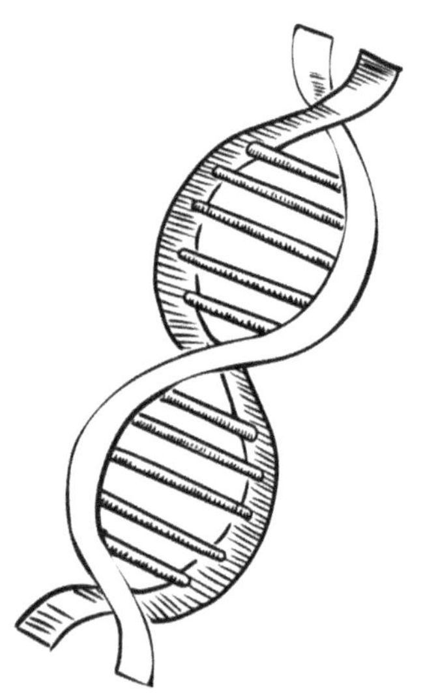

Chain reaction

What if I told you
that there's no such thing as random?
Everything experienced
is just a chain reaction
and experience itself
is just a vector that we're trapped in
Appearances are more than they seem
and as they happen
Happiness is a frequency:
Breeze in the aspens
Being cool isn't as cool as it seems
when trees are saplings
They need so much more
than good nurturing
They need a habitat
that presents them with consistency
You see we're battling
a fight between those out there who lead
without a battle plan
and those who often accept defeat
before the battles end
and nobody can win when we feed
off of the silver tongued
who show us what they want us to see:
The worlds an evil one

Engagement with fools

Demoralized into picking
what sort of carcass to consume
We all captivate on pain we feel
but can't rectify the wound
Whole world wound up tightly
and most have showed up too soon
to enjoy fruits of our labors
of engagement with the fools
Look into my eyes and tell me
last time that you slept
on a bed that's not your own
with an odd pillow under neck
It's the feeling I feel often
no matter where my head may land
Underhanded actors acting
in ways I don't understand
Oh so impolite yet we engage with politics
for we are strangers in a forest
on a trail in some respect
Some prefer the taste of your flesh
and will take all they can get
So we weaponized ourselves
then did things that we regret
Now we watch it boil over
all the tribes have battle cries
While the green backed blue faced monster
shows some skin and bats it's eyes
It's apocalyptic opera
no prophet could have prophesied

So be sure to like and comment
and go ahead and just subscribe
to our inevitable downfall
There will be no crown or prize
We are children on an island
this is lord of the flies

Views

Curtains rise I sit inside
a box that's filled with liquid
of an unknown origin
unveiled by dancing women
Arms behind my back
I have been shackled in securely
I'm an emcee escape artist
but it's you who's in the prison
Keys inside my mind
My private jet:
the astral plane
I've been scoping out some islands
just to rest my tired frame
but the fatal flaw in circumstance:
I'm boxed up somewhere drowning
for somebody's entertainment
or to keep me locked in silence
I don't let it bug me though
just close both my eyelids
as I preserve my last oxygen
and prepare for the violence:
Then psionic waves erupt
the windows crack and shatter
hematomas everywhere
erupted screams and laughter
Audience in front row is both soaking in the spectacle
and soaked in liquid from my cell
Respectively detestable
I'm best at going hard
They should have never ever tested
Ones I leave alive are ones
I leave to propagate that lesson

This just in on CSPAN
It's a slaughter there's explosions
They would have called in choppers
but they're scared to get in close
Seems that anything within a block has
been reduced to ashes
So here's Tom with the weather
Please just stay in
till this passes

Rose Woman

Been knocked down
Been chewed up
Been spit out
Been through enough
Been growing since you been small
and since then you've been tough
Misogyny has been sold to all
and since then you've felt smothered
Want to reveal your soul to all
but in fear it's still covered
Rose girl you're budding
with thorns for protection
they want to get your treasure
and take it don't let them
Your mind is a wonder
your soul and your body
are vessel and liquid
and all is worth watching
allow yourself to push through all
the hurt and pain and the sorrow
The harder today they say is the way
to longer and stronger tomorrows
Those bullies may come out to try
To take and to break and to torture
But in the story you're living
girlfriend, you're the hero the fortune
It's in you without you we're lacking creation
Most pleasant invention inventing and waiting
I hope that you feel all the words that I'm laying
Fragrance you put out is a lot to take in

I know that most things
are better shown than spoken
You are essential energy
Need you rose woman
You rise up, you fight hard,
you look good, you love deep
You're constant, consistent
You rose out the concrete

Rose woman
Love yourself
I know that you been through hell
Growing out the cement
They demand that you bend
you'll be last to laugh
they'll see you bloom in the end

ameri-kkk

Every cops a bastard with their finger on
trigger
Hit the streets till they respect us
Talking summer or winter
We all know that they been lyin
Turn their roar to a whimper
Burn down every single precinct
Wish it was all that simple
Been wearing masks and armor
like we think it's October
Constant escalating tactics
Urban wars never over
Could someone that's without sin
podcast to the next stoner?
ameri-KKK
Protecting its white property owners

Heavens close

Hope that somebodies been takin notes
Naked and waiting I lay enclosed
in a cocoon of my latest quotes
They protect me as change evolves
Transform to slime to sprout my wings
I'm more than a moth to flame it seems
Running from heat and painful stings
of wading through the city streets
For when out there I am exposed
to racist hateful
homophobe bros
We need to rise above it all
but truth be told
we're losing hope
Mother, Daughter, Holy Ghost
Madam Magdalena doing most
Full arena of the folks
who look on disgusted as she is broken
Born of dust, and sick of dirt
Breathing smoke; consuming earth
Sycophants sit and dance on top of her
warm corpse
for a chance to get more popular
Fortunate for the ignorant and
woe be to beholders
But which wretch rules the wasteland
once it's only smolders?
who will live to sweeten up the tale we tell each other
of the times we had before we fell
When we thought that we were clever

Leave a lot or leave a corpse
we all one day get leveled
and the evil that we've been of course
will still remain in echoes
Poltergeists and ghosts of thoughts
attach to us like specters
Cleansing self of all the fog
is what love and self-respect is

Climbing tingle up your spine
The coaster peaks crescendo
More to life than screens
and playing games
We aren't Nintendo
You have imagination sure
but don't be a pretender
There is more to see
than we've been shown
in magic handheld windows

Cross faded

Social media the crucifix
we're now cross faded
take some drugs
put them in the mix
If offered we will take it
Act famous and then take some pics
then pretend you don't hate it
It's a misdirect with no success
that only sates the brain dead

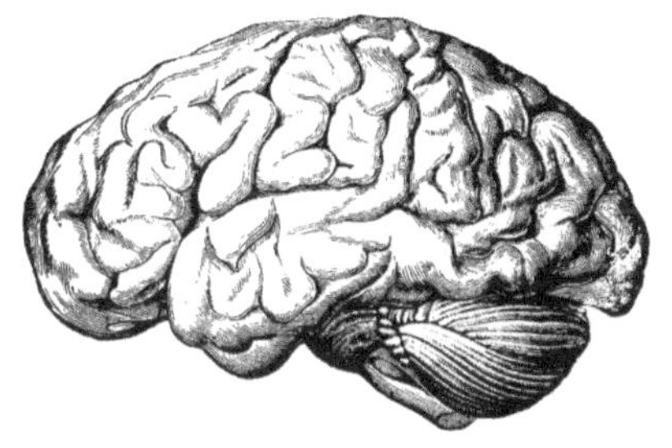

melded

Wanna melt into you, lover
Watch you melt all over me
What we feel once we are melded
we will then allow to be
Wanna writhe in heat together
Wanna breathe you as you breathe
Wanna make with you a rhythm
out of all our make believe
I just love to touch you deeply
and to see you at your seams
and to then show to you my edges
and swap back and forth, our dreams
with an effervescent presence
Let's bask in our harmony
as we head toward the future
What sort of music will we be?

Belly of the Monster

Rounding corners I can feel it everywhere we go
Rationalizations for the ways we act irrational
Actually waiting for a savior we don't even know
its all more than make believe
so yippee ki-yay here go
Strong believer in the river that is flowing out
of each and every conscious thing
that seems to roam about
Solid matter is the aether and it's freaking out
organizing where it's going
we ain't even keeping up
Feel resistance from the belly of the monster
You're it's armor so what is your response here?
Know this girl she got ghosts that still haunt her
Catch her lying to herself
saying that no one wants her
Met a kid who just lost it to drugs
The more that you do
you become what you does
World can kill us off
and it shouldn't be trusted
Now they're with the angels, boy
my buddy got dusted
Call me a buzzkill or call me a bastard
on egg shells and glass we been walking
it's backwards

Tired of all of the last chances, last words
like last year was the first time
we laid down bad patterns
as a collective now let's start a little groovin
Progression is the dance
oblivious to approval
Justice doesn't come
just cause we seek improvement
but it never comes if we just stand
in idle movement
Shoe fits well? better walk a mile in it
I will not stop rhyming until I am finished
with my point
your wallet can be full of spinach
but if you keep it for yourself
then you suffer malnutrition

Eventually: believing

Maybe fungus made up consciousness
to propagate its species?
Maybe apes ate of the mushrooms
that they found under cow feces?
Maybe this whole world is a dream
brought forth by what we're perceiving?
Doesn't matter where we're going
We'll eventually: believing

Maybe there's more to the world we're in
than what our senses show us?
From the cradle to the waiting grave
doesn't every kid or grown-up
have to have at least a little faith
their prayers don't go to no one;
even if they're only in your brain
when times are sad or solemn?

Some may call it God, or spirits,
Mother Earth if you're fancy
Tesla knew harmonic resonance
was the planet's waiting answer
Through an energetic process
that the cosmos cares not cancel;
are we not walking talking proof
of thermodynamical transfer?

So miraculous in nature
that it's built in we dismiss it
When it's gone though or burnt up
We'll cry out on how we all miss it
For by living selfishly
instead of in cycles permitted;
we'll face extinction before answers
to the questions I've presented

Hope for rain

Pulled into my pupils the whole spectrum of light
Filtered down to images by software inside
Rewritten when recalled again; a place out of time
You could call it our memories I call it divine
Answer to the calling feel the web like a spider
Wider chakras open up
the more you will find here
Feel ancestral energy
you have been put right here
By all who came before you
All who lived fought and died here
Search inside with your third eye
There's gifts you've been given
Pick a number now that's between 9 and eleven
Trauma is a part of us it's what we're attending
and there's ten thousand things to break us
or to deal with the tension
Cry out for attention
or give a hand for lending
Find a stranger you're alike and then
get to the friending
If this is the apocalypse
And our world is ending
You should mind to what your focus is
real life or pretending
What's a drop of water
to a drought in the desert?
Doubt leads to disruption
we regret that we get hurt
Being a neighbor or friend
May not get you to trending
but it's the way to better days
and to happier endings

Rain after a fire
We are cooling relief
So model self as dedicated
and then choose it to be
Our home's trying to reject us
as we all try to flee
from the fact that to in the grand scheme
we're as small as a flea
Can't ride into the sunset
on the dead horse we're beating
Some sights can stop the heart
but the trees keep on breathing
and before we each fall down
on our way to our leaving
there's a lot we have to grow
in that much we're agreeing
So sing along and follow
all the wretched and cretins
who will never get around
to your Rectangular feelings
cross-eyed they defend
our "liberties" and our "freedoms"
generation built on genocide
and star spangled stealing
Un-indoctrinate yourself
or be more than willing
to let go of broken yesterday's
and accept the healing
offered in redemption
and the debt we're fulfilling
by trying not to hate ourselves
Cuz we're only just children

To the few people without whom this book
would be impossible:

Thank you so much for the light you bring into my life and all the love and warmth! Thank you for the inspiration, the laughs, and the heart ache and tears! I'm still learning how to be well out here and always will be and I can't even begin to express my gratitude for the ways you round me off and keep me sane. We are only as good as the company we keep and I know that I'm amazing because you assure me of it. Thank you thank you from the bottom of my heart for your continued love and support as our journey through life together unfolds in cascading waves of raw emotion and experience.
I love you, always.

Warren